My Life in FRANCE

Patience Coster

Peachtree

New York

Published in 2015 by Cavendish Square Publishing, LLC
243 5th Avenue, Suite 136, New York, NY 10016

First Edition

CPSIA Compliance Information: Batch #WW15CSQ

All websites were available and accurate when this book was sent to press.

Library of Congress Cataloging-in-Publication Data

Coster, Patience.
My life in France / Patience Coster.
pages cm. — (Children of the world)
Includes index.
ISBN 978-1-50260-046-2 (hardcover) ISBN 978-1-50260-047-9 (paperback)
ISBN 978-1-50260-279-4 (ebook)
1. France—Social life and customs—Juvenile literature. 2. Children—France—Juvenile literature. I. Title.

DC17.C695 2015
944—dc23

2014028062

Editor: Joe Harris
Designer: Ian Winton

All photography courtesy of Alain Pitton / Demotix / Corbis

Printed in the United States of America

Contents

7:30 AM

My Day Begins

Salut! My name is Louise. I am ten years old. I live with my mom, dad, and little sister Corinne in Damazan, a village in southwest France.

There are around 1,300 people in Damazan. My family lives in an old farmhouse on the edge of the village.

Louise says ...

We have bread, yogurt, and hot chocolate for breakfast.

Corinne is drinking hot chocolate from her bowl.

When breakfast is finished, I brush my hair and tie it back for school.

My Country

France is a large country in Western Europe. It has a **population** of around sixty-six million people. Damazan is in the Lot-et-Garonne (lot-teh-gair-on) region. It is a beautiful, hilly part of France named after the Lot and Garonne rivers.

8:00 AM

Going to School

Corinne and I go to the *école élémentaire (ay-coal ay-lay-mahn-tair)*, or primary school. The school takes both boys and girls and there is no uniform so we can wear our normal clothes.

We study French, math, geography, history, art, and a foreign language. I am learning English.

On the way to school I meet my friend Nicole. We have known each other since we were little.

Speaking French

Here in France, we speak French. French is an important language in many other countries, including Switzerland, Belgium, Canada, and many African countries.

Registration

My school is called Groupe Scolaire de Damazan. State schools in France are **secular**. This means there is no religious teaching or morning worship.

Louise says ...

Before school some of us get together to rehearse for the end-of-year show.

To start the day, instead of attendance, we have registration. We each have to answer *"Oui" (we)* – meaning "Yes" – when our name is called.

Types of Schools

In France, children start primary school at the age of six. We go on to *collège (coal-ledge)* or middle school at age eleven. From the age of fifteen we go to ***lycée*** (leh-say) or high school. There are two main types of *lycée*– general and technical.

Morning Classes

I am in class CM1. We are getting ready to go to middle school, so we take lots of tests.

There are eighteen students in my class. We have to work quietly during lesson time.

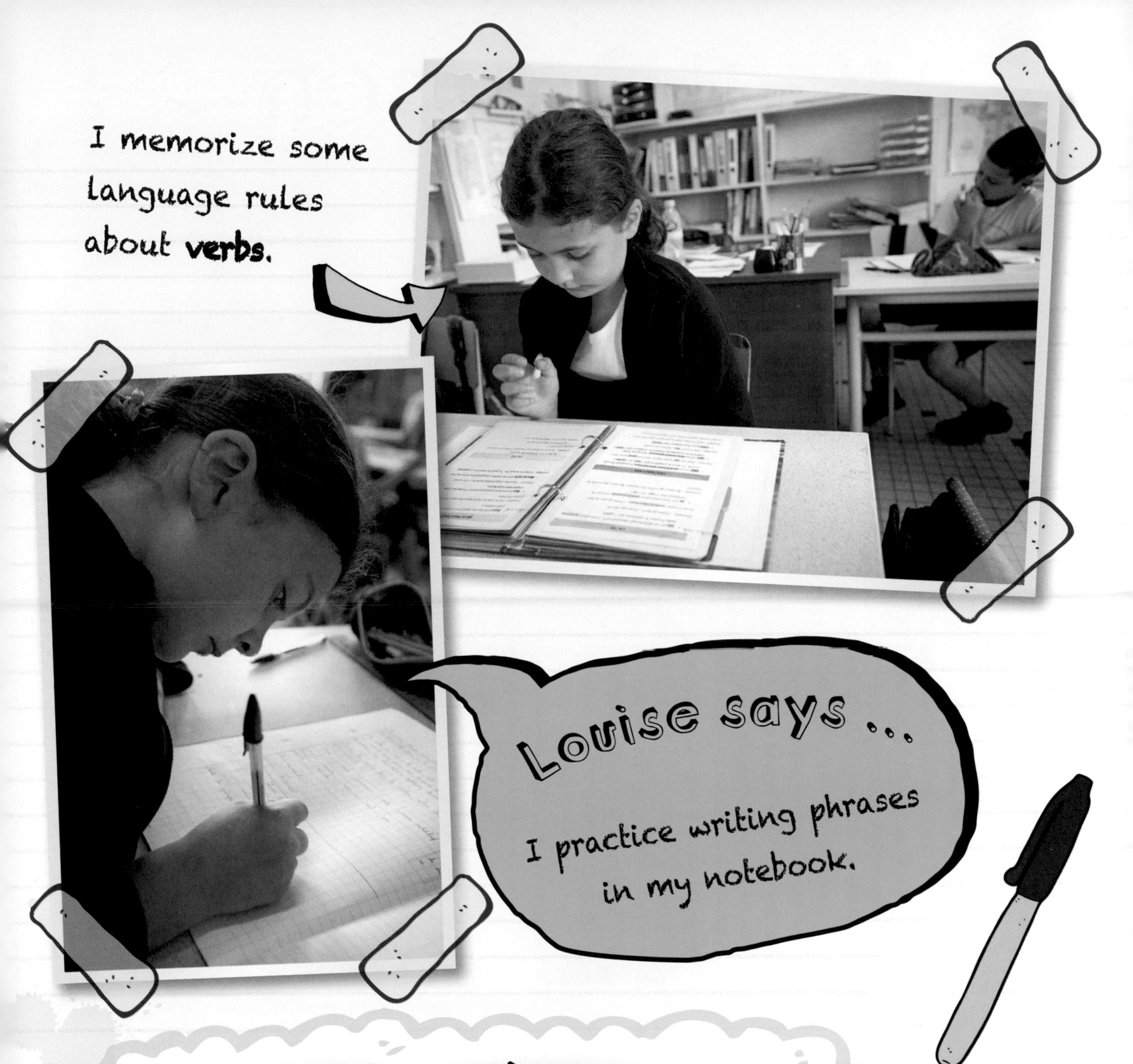

Education

There are five classes in primary school – CP, CE1, CE2, CM1, and CM2. CP is **preparatory** class, CE is **elementary** class, and CM is middle class. The last two classes prepare students for middle school.

Math Lesson

After breaktime, which lasts fifteen minutes, we have a math test. We are working on addition, division, multiplication, and subtraction.

Louise says ...

Math is my favorite subject.

I finish the test quickly so I'm allowed to read a book.

8 = 15

2 x 9 = 18

Afterward, our teacher, Madame Girard, gives us a *défi mathémathique (day-fee mat-uh-mah-teek)* – a math challenge. We work in teams of three. The first group to finish with the right answers gets a reward.

The Importance of Math

The French emperor Napoleon Bonaparte believed that math would make France a successful nation. Today, many French people still say that math is the most important subject in school. Many famous mathematicians are French.

Lunchtime

We have a two-hour break for lunch. Today Corinne is staying at school to eat in the cafeteria. I walk home on my own.

I wash my hands while Mom makes lunch. I'm really hungry after working so hard!

Louise says ...
Mmm, this **croque-monsieur** (croak-muh-sur) is delicious!

A croque-monsieur is a grilled ham and cheese sandwich.

French Food

The French diet consists mainly of fresh vegetables, meats, and cheeses. French people eat their main meal in the evening, having often just a sandwich or **quiche** for lunch. Famous dishes include onion soup and thin pancakes called ***crêpes***.

1:30 PM

Back to School

After lunch, I walk back to school so that I arrive half an hour before class starts.

We play the sparrowhawk game then rehearse some more for the school show.

It's time to start lessons again, so we go back to the classroom.

Sparrowhawk Game

For the sparrowhawk game, one child is the hawk and stands in the middle of the playground. When the hawk calls out "I'm coming!" the other children run across the playground. If the hawk catches them, they become sparrowhawks too.

Afternoon Classes

In the afternoon we have geography. We are learning about the different landscape features of France.

Louise says ...

If there is anything we don't understand, Madame Girard explains it to us.

Then we have a French **grammar** lesson. Grammar is the correct way of speaking and writing. In France we think this is very important. Today we are learning about **punctuation**.

I get up to answer some questions in front of the class, using the interactive whiteboard.

Mont Blanc

The biggest mountain in Europe is in the French **Alps** on the Italian border. Called Mont Blanc (French for "White Mountain"), it is 15,781 ft (4,810 meters) high. A 7-mile- (11-kilometer-) long tunnel through the mountain connects France with Italy.

Homework

School is finished for the day – but I still have an hour of homework to do. We work hard in France!

I eat some **baguette** with cherry jam before starting on my homework.

Tomorrow I have tests in geography and history. My mom helps me review.

The French Revolution

The most famous event in French history is the French Revolution. In 1789, the ordinary people rose up against the richest people in the country. They removed the **monarchy** (the king and his family) from power. Many people who disagreed with the revolution were put to death with a machine called the **guillotine**.

Baking a Cake

Now for some downtime! I love baking, so today I'm going to make a salted caramel cake.

I need eggs, butter, flour, and sugar to start.

Corinne comes to help. We need to blend all the ingredients together until the mixture is soft and creamy.

Louise says ...

Stirring the cake mix makes my arm tired – but it will be worth it!

Pâtisseries

A *pâtisserie (pah-tea-sree)* is a bakery that specializes in making fancy pastries and sweets. There is a *pâtisserie* in almost every town in France. French pastry chefs train for a long time. This shows in the quality of their cakes, which are often works of art to look at as well as delicious to eat!

6:00 PM

Music Practice

While the cake is baking, I practice music. I am learning to play the oboe.

I have lessons at a music school in Tonneins, a nearby town.

Louise says ...

Learning how to blow into the mouthpiece of the oboe is quite tricky.

When I've finished practicing I send some messages to my friends online.

Music in France

Many famous composers (writers of music) come from France. People all over the world love the music of Hector Berlioz, Maurice Ravel, and Claude Debussy. *Chanson française*, a style of solo singing with a very long history, is still popular in France. Great artists include Edith Piaf, Juliette Greco, Charles Aznavour, and Jacques Brel.

Playtime

Before dinner, we go outside to play. We are lucky to have a big garden and to live in the countryside. There are lots of trees and places to play.

Corinne and I play a game of catch. The most popular sport in France is soccer, which we call football.

Louise says ...

We are eating outside tonight, so I bring out the salted caramel cake we have made.

Then we shower and get changed into our pajamas.

Boules

A game called *boules (bool)* is very popular all over France. It is played with heavy metal balls on sandy ground. The goal is to throw or roll your ball as close as possible to a small ball, which is the target.

8:00 PM

Dinner and Bedtime

For dinner we have an **omelette**, salad, and melon. We save the cake for last – everyone loves it!

I brush my teeth before going to bed.

My bedroom is snug and cozy. I take one last look at my book for the test tomorrow, then I turn off the light.

Rural Life

Until the early twentieth century, at least two-thirds of French people lived in the countryside. Most people lived in **communities** of less than 100 people. Today less than a quarter of the French population lives in the countryside.

Glossary

Alps A European mountain range stretching across the countries of France, Switzerland, Italy, Austria, Slovenia, and Germany.

baguette A long, thin loaf of bread, usually white, with a crunchy crust.

communities Groups of people living in the same place.

crêpes Thin pancakes usually served smeared with jam or filled with a savory, creamy sauce.

croque-monsieur A ham and cheese sandwich, served hot (fried or grilled).

elementary Introductory or basic.

grammar The rules and structure of a language.

guillotine A machine with a heavy blade, designed to drop suddenly, used for beheading people.

lycée A French secondary school.

monarchy A system of government which has a king or queen as head of state.

omelette A dish of beaten eggs fried in a frying pan, often served with a savory filling of cheese or mushrooms.

population The total number of people living in a place, such as a country.

preparatory A school for very young children which prepares them for elementary school.

punctuation Marks in writing, for example, comma, period, and semi-colon, used to separate sentences and make meaning clear.

quiche A savory tart with a filling made of egg custard, often flavored with vegetables, cheese, and/or ham.

secular Not religious.

verbs Words used to describe actions, such as run, walk, swim, etc.

Further Information

Websites

kids.nationalgeographic.com/explore/countries/france.html
Geography, nature, people, culture, government, economy, and history.

www.bbc.co.uk/learningzone/clips/daily-school-routines-in-french
Video clip featuring Papo the parrot, who learns what life is like at a school in France.

http://dinolingo.com/blog/2011/05/04/french-culture
Fun facts for kids – food, music, language, and more.

www.discoverfrance.net
Culture, history, language, travel, and more.

www.kids-world-travel-guide.com/france-facts.html
Facts researched by and for children.

Further Reading

Finnie, Sue, and Daniele Bourdais. *Young Reporter in France series.* London, England: Franklin Watts, 2014.

Ganeri, Anita. *France: A Benjamin Blog and His Inquisitive Dog Guide.* Chicago, IL: Raintree, 2014.

Peppas, Lynn. *Cultural Traditions in France.* New York, NY: Crabtree Publishing, 2014.

Powell, Jillian. *Looking at Countries: France.* London, England: Franklin Watts, 2010.

Savery, Annabel. *Been There! France.* London, England: Franklin Watts, 2004.

Thomson, Ruth. *Countries: France.* London, England: Wayland, 2013.

Index